The Next Best Version of the Woman I am Becoming

By Barbara Jean Caballero

ISBN: 978-1-4276-5187-7
Library of Congress Control Number: 2011929207

Contents

Introduction

The "next best version of the woman I am becoming" is an idea from Donald Neale Walsh. It has become one of my "Barbaraism's" the phrases and words that I live by.

The first version of this came from college where I learned that most of us reach less than 3% of our potential. I vowed that no one would ever be able to say that about me; that I would spend my life exploring my potential, stretching and reaching for more – to be more and do more, not to have more. Getting things, looking good, keeping up appearances has never appealed to me. I want to be remembered for who I am and what I do, not for what I have.

The class was about goals and particularly written goals. The author claimed that those who write down and review their goals regularly accomplish far more than the rest of us. I may have carried that to an extreme. I set yearly goals, then monthly goals. I review those goals regularly, change or move them as necessary and add new ones. I like to have a yearly theme and a monthly theme. I like to do daily, weekly, monthly and yearly evaluations of where I have been and where I am going.

As I have learned to make "living in the moment' and 'practice' part of my skill sets, I find myself more able to see what is happening and give meaning to what I am experiencing and learning. What do I mean by "practice"? When I get frustrated and ask for simple how-to steps, especially in the realm of spiritual growth, I get told, "practice". Just try, do the best you know in the moment. As we do more and more practice, we learn what works for us. We find better choices, we notice what happens next, we witness.

I can say that giving up "littleness" is one of my growth areas, but it is not a class I can graduate from, but rather an ongoing practice. I am confronted over and over with opportunities to practice giving up littleness. Or perhaps I should say that I am learning to stand in my own power. That is the affirmative side of giving up littleness. A variation on this theme is giving up the need to feel heard. That, of course, goes all the way back to Stephen R Covey and his guidance to seek first to understand and then to be understood. I still often revert to the childish need to be heard first, which then turns off whoever I want to hear me since he feels threatened by my demands. So, I am learning to stop, breathe, be still, listen. Then I can feel my hurt, my own pain, can see it has come from a long life and can give myself the love and hearing that I need. I can feel the feelings through and let them go.

Another important piece of all of this came from a retreat where I learned to give up high expectations of others, to receive what was there for me, to honor the beautiful moments and the gifts to release the rest, blow it away like so much chaff. I get so much more out of my retreats with this attitude, but I must constantly remind myself, because judging slinks in so quietly, that we hardly know it has arrived again. And it is time to practice, to witness, to let go.

Frontispiece

It Is So

Today is the first day of the rest of my life.
I awake with a smile honoring the quiet,
Entering into communion with my Heavenly Father.
I listen for the words that guide my day
Filling my heart with gratitude and love.
I set my intentions, order my plans.
Refreshed, relaxed, I am eager to flow
Out into the upcoming adventures.
To make connections, encourage, delight.
To fill my spaces with laughter and possibility.
My stepping stones are the differences I make.
My wings are the differences others make.
I am warmed by opportunities to get involved,
To dance through the challenges
With heartfelt listening, attention and acceptance
Knowing at day's end I have done my best,
I will sleep well in the arms of love.

Next Higher Version

"Always Becoming" is the name of a display in front of the American Indian Museum, a part of the Smithsonian Museum Complex in Washington, D.C. It is made mostly of natural mud so the weather changes it over time.

We, too, are always becoming. Today's choices lead to tomorrow's becoming. So our task is to choose wisely, to embrace all that is beautiful and wonderful.

Anthony Robbins teaches CANI – constant and never-ending improvement. I seek to plan ways to use more of my potential, to be more, to do more.

A Meditation

In this present moment
I breathe in and out.
I seek stillness.
I become attuned to the one.
Peacefully, I accept.
I love.
I am grateful.
I listen.
As guidance comes
I ponder and question,
Noticing if there
Is more clarity,
If the next step
Feels right,
Moves me higher
To the next best version
Of the woman
I am becoming.

The Next Best Version

Everyday produces challenges
Designed to provoke response.
It is my job to choose:
Will I react?
Or step up to the next best version
Be clarifying and waiting,
Taking it to the spirit,
Acting only on inspiration.
In pondering the challenge
I see more clearly,
Identify deeper meanings.
Then, when the time is ripe,
I respond from my heart,
Stepping up to the next best version
Of the woman I am becoming.

In My Power

Coming from home
In my Heavenly Father's presence
Stepping out into
The beauty of the day.
Still contemplative, grateful
I am in awe of all
That surrounds me,
Prepared to step into my power.
I see deeply.
The world here resonates the happiness
Of like-minded people.
Stepping up to greater possibilities -
Connecting, sharing, accepting what is
But holding great visions
Working together
Building synergies

Mountain Dancer

Uriah says that mountain dreamer
Is Indian for "one who pushes the edges".
I like that. I've adopted my own version:
Henceforth, I shall be known as
"Mountain Dancer"
I shall dance across mountains,
Push the clouds away.
I shall sing aloud and make people smile.
I shall seek random acts of kindness
That make my heart dance.
My smiles will cover the earth,
Moving from face-to-face
Like party streamers filling the skies and
I will laugh out loud.

Describing Myself In Three Words Or Less

I am.
What I envision, believe, value,
Accept, see is what I am becoming.
My goal is to step up
To the next best version
Of the woman I am becoming.
I can.
I can make a difference.
I can find time and space for bliss.
I can love, empower, offer light,
Share experiences,
Delight in the moment,
Expand my consciousness.
I will
Listen and learn
For new ways to do better, be more.
I will hear the stories others tell.
I will recognize diversity,
Accept the grace
That surrounds, uplifts me.

Intention

I start each day with a daily reading. Usually this points me to an intent. If not, I read other materials until I come to the truth I will center on for the day. This intent becomes a point of alignment, a way to move back to center when life gets hectic or I seem scattered.

Then I get quiet and listen for a bit of inspiration and guidance. Spirit guides me to the next step, my next choice.

At the end of day, I look back, check the alignment ,and extract the deeper meanings, the lessons of all that has happened.

One retreat leader suggested we start each day with the phrase –"This is what I have to say to you". Then write and see what comes. Her poetry comes from these early morning meditations

Intentions give us the lift to move beyond our "possibility base camp".

New Beginnings

I love the early morning hours,
The quiet, the peacefulness,
The time to consider, to listen.
I love the first fingers of light
Signaling a new dawn, a new day,
A new beginning.
Father guides me
As I set my intent
Prepare for action.

The dust and grit
Of the day's activities
Collect,
Sometimes weighing me down.
But breath, heart, laughter
Lift me again
'Til evening when I look back,
Count my blessings, my successes,
Savor lessons learned, joys received,
Lay my head down
In the hammock of night, and
Release both intent and regret.

What I Think About Myself

This is a wonderful new day;
Precious moments given to be savored.
I like me! I like the way I start my days.

I like reading great ideas and setting
An intention for the day.
I like planning and tracking successes.

I like looking for ways to make a difference,
Random acts of kindness.
I like the increased awareness they provide.

I like taking time out
To watch a pair of cardinals
To walk around a lake.

I like being married
Doing things together, helping each other,
Cuddling and touching, talking and sharing.

I like savoring the moments
Recognizing and acknowledging happiness.
Going deeper, seeking essence.
I like stringing the jewels of each day
To admire again
And letting go of what did not quite work out.

Intention

Vision sighs into intention
Opening I receive
Heavenly Father frames my day
Prepares the way
Early morning I take his hand
Watching dawn spread across the sky
I smile, moved to motion,
I dance. Quieting, I write.
Planning and prioritizing set the mood
Listening defines the importance
Tugged again to my feet
Skipping out the door
To meet the challenges and opportunities.

A Masterpiece

I am making a masterpiece of this day,
Rising to greet the dawn with my green tea.
Taking in the beauty, the light, the scents.
I breathe in calm and serenity.
With prayer and meditation I set my intention
And am aware and sensitive
To others' intentions and body language.
I clarify with open ended questions,
Listening deeply, appreciatively.
I am open to all possibilities.
I am strong and flexible, choosing consciously.
I enjoy the current activity
Sipping the nectar of the moment
Extracting meaning, joy, depth,
Understanding. I seek win/win situations.
I discover, ponder, explore,
Accept and love.
I am making a masterpiece of this day.

Yesterday I Lost

Twenty-four hours
That I can never get back again.

Sight of my carefully set intention
Those things have a way of drifting off

Time I wanted to spend meditating,
But not really, since I was journaling

And for me that is a great meditation
So what I lost was really a false judgment.

Today I found

Twenty-four bright shiny new hours
Begging me to come out and play

A new intention and the ability
To return to center and reclaim

My beautiful intention.
Journaling helped me decide what was important.

Without self criticisms
I felt like I could fly.

Anything is possible as I lift off from my "possibility base camp".

Centering

I find that starting my day from a quiet place in communion with my Heavenly Father helps me have a better day. I like to spend some time in prayer and mediation early in the morning. Prayer is my conversation, while meditation is giving Heavenly Father my attention so that he can teach and guide me.

As I go through my day, if I pause and go back to that center, that place of peace and quiet, then I remember what I am about and am more able to hear the quiet guidance. I am able to let go of the ego which wants to take over and defend and straighten out the world.

In this quiet place, I am able to make better choices, to seek the best path for whatever situation I find myself in. I am able to look more carefully, open my eyes to other perspectives, understand more deeply.

Beginnings

Peace begins with me
And radiates outward.
I take the time
To be at peace with God,
At peace with who I am,
Who I am becoming.
I find peace in my surroundings –
My home, my garden, my community.
I become peaceful in my relationships,
Seeing beauty and possibility
In every person I interact with.
Peace is built one moment at a time
With our thoughts, our smiles, our hands.
We are "at one" each with the other,
And it is well.

"Aaah"

I am still.
I focus on my breath.
I am grateful.
I see beauty, love.
All things are possible.
I choose, focus.
Go with the flow,
Savoring each moment,
Feeling the feeling,
Learning the lessons.
I create my dreams
Give them form.
I arise, infused with
Energy and excitement,
Letting it all be.
This, or something better
According to God's will.

Temenos

A sacred center
Beyond right and wrong
A place of "being"
A personal sanctuary.
From this center,
I prepare by letting go,
By being still and listening,
By learning to hear
Words of guidance.

My journal is the point of entry,
The "idea hoard",
A place to accept my feelings,
To explore, discover,
To return at day's end,
Extract meaning, beauty, delight,
To evaluate, take in the lessons,
Breathe in the silences, the love.

Blanket Of Love

See spirit
As a warm fluffy blanket.
When you need strength,
Enfold yourself in that blanket.
Feel its warmth.
Personalize it
With the colors, texture and
Softness you like best.
Within God's blanket of love
Look at what you are feeling
With complete acceptance.
Let the feeling lighten and
Slip away, so that
You rest in calm,
Sweet stillness,
Knowing you are loved.

The Promise Of A New Day

My heart overflows with gratitude
For the promise of each day,
For the peaceful moments
Of beginning anew.

Time to be still and listen,
To ponder this new day,
To open my eyes
To a deeper, wider view.

My heart overflows with gratitude
For healing and health,
For the ability to move,
To stretch and grow.

I love the feeling
Of deep breaths
Filling and
Expanding my lungs.

Fresh fruit and berries,
Whole grains,
The milk of life
Filling me, preparing me to go forth

To open to all that is,
To learn and grow,
To respond to what is,
To pay it forward, make a difference.

Called

Signals of which I am
Only dimly aware
Call me to a new level of awareness,
To a sacred frame of mind,
A communion with something bigger,
A call to form, to materialize a new me.
My unfolding requires
That I be in dialogue
With whatever is calling me.
I put on a new lens
To see my life
As a process of calls and responses
There is a certainty
That it all makes sense.

Going On Retreat

A 2:00 A.M threshold crossing gave me time
To move more slowly, to adjust
To a different way of being.
Before dawn, I set my intent
To seek, to acknowledge inspiration.
I read of how great words can inspire
And I receive a pertinent message
Proving that all is again according to plan.
Pushed to stand in that awareness
To take time for prayer and meditation.
I seek better ways to express
Knowledge from those on the path ahead of me.
I was counseled 'Be patient. A breakthrough is coming."
Go inside and ask. Get your direction from your Source.
And so I have arrived.
Ready and happy to welcome whatever golden nuggets
Are here for my open heart to absorb.
I pray for conscious awareness of
A perfect learning that already is: the 'quiddity',
The essence of this perfect moment.
I go into the stillness and ask. pause, listen, let it be.
Receive, acknowledge,
Write it down for future ponderings
Until my very own jewel
Is polished into a multitude of facets,
Sparkling meanings that glow with interior light
Prisming off into rainbows of gratitude.

Presence

I want to live my life one moment at a time. I find joy in being present to the current moment – a child's laugh, a sunset, a beautiful song.

And yet I miss many moments in looking back at what has passed, playing the "what if" game or worrying about what might happen in the future. This is not savoring wonderful memories or making plans that set my intentions on a path toward fulfillment, but rather the thoughts that I stir in an effort to change the past or future. The successful way to change the future is by changing the choice I make in the current moment.

Welcoming sensation helps ground me in the moment: fresh berries straight from a bush, the meadowlark's tune, noticing differences in tree trunk textures, the movement from dark to dawn. I am present to the beauty, the intensity of the moment. I am filled, centered. Gratitude wells up and bursts forth. Thank-you. YES

Cracking It Open

Opening a single moment
With my enjoyment,
My awareness, my presence.
Revealing the extraordinary,
Time to receive,
To smile in gratitude,
To build a memory
That will continue to warm
Throughout my days and nights.
Today I am precious and
Rare and awake.
I will say what I feel
I will follow my curiosity
I will love and
Bless each event, each moment.

On High Roads

I walk on high roads,
Open doors to anywhere
Catch the sunlight
Dance with the breezes.
I cherish things worth stopping for.
I catch soft smiles,
Sift laughter through my fingers,
Smooth the wrinkles
With a kind touch.
I memorize precious moments,
Touch you with my eyes,
Stretch out my hand.

The Poet As An Amplifier

What makes a poet?
Eyes that marvel
At the blue of the sky,
The raindrop spattered leaf
And a child's small hand.

What makes a poet?
Feet which follow
Curiosity,
Feet that run
And play.

What makes a poet?
Knees that crack and moan
Watering a plant, weeding,
Bending in prayer
Before the wonder of it all.

What makes a poet?
Hands that write
What has been seen,
Heard and felt.
Hands that reach out.

What makes a poet?
A tender heart
Where secrets are held,
Then pondered
And shared.

I Can

Today I am choice
In the silence I am
Listening. An idea comes.
I consider ways
To move it into action
For the best good of all.
I want love, connection, joy.
At essence we are
So much alike,
Dealing with the same issues
In the best ways we know.
Nourishing myself,
I see the beauty,
The possibilities in others
I listen with an open heart,
Feel the feelings, connect.
I move into my own potential,
Inviting others along
Into their potentials.

Pearls Of The Present

Admiring and accepting
The pearls of the present,
Allowing their beauty
To sink deeply into my consciousness
Till I overflow
Into thanksgiving,
Till I step lightly
Into the flow
Of each new moment,
Excited by
All possibilities.

Transforming The Moment

Any turn in the wheel of sensation
Has the power to crystallize and
Transform this moment.
Berries fresh picked from the vine,
A field of robins,
The lapping of water on the shoreline.
One moment this life is moving along
The next there is a stop, a pause,
A realization.
A full blown gratitude engulfs you.
The moment imprints itself upon your life
And suddenly nothing is the same….
Still you go on doing,
But now with a new lift in your step,
A song in your heart,
A gleam in your eye,
A smile slipping out from hiding.

Acceptance

One author writes that acceptance is the intersection of mindfulness and gentle self-compassion. Present, I look and see. This is what is, without judgment. In clearly defining the moment, I open myself to more choices. The thank-you accepts, appreciates draws meaning. Then "YES" chooses the highest choice and acts moving me into the next moment, the next acceptance, the next choice. Till at the end of the day I review it all, accept the lessons, the gifts and release all the rest with the setting of the sun.

What in this moment is amazing? What are the gifts?

Wherever I am, I can connect. A smile, laughter – moments of delight that ripple out into the world creating waves of happiness.

Another part of acceptance is "letting go", letting go of expectations and taking what comes with an open heart. Finding the gold and blowing the rest away as so much"chaff".

Beggar's Bowl

There is a lovely pottery bowl
That sits on my coffee table empty
Reminding me to be open
To whatever comes my way
To accept, savor, enjoy.

Several years ago
I attended a bread and soup dinner.
We bought pottery bowls
And were served soup and bread.
It was a lovely dinner,
Surrounded by new friends and old,
Knowing that the money we raised
Was going to support a soup kitchen
For those who, for the moment,
Had less than we did.

Sue Ann Bender talks of
The beggar's bowl;
Of approaching each day
As monks do
Taking their bowls out
And accepting whatever
They were given
As their sustenance
For that day.
With heartfelt gratitude.

Seeing

It is a great day!
My part is seeing it as such,
Accepting and appreciating
A song lyric
"Some people wait all their lives
For a moment like this."
A change in perspective –
What in this moment is so amazing?
What brings me to delight, laughter?
What makes my eyes shine,
My heart fly?
What bold act feels really great?

I AM

I am a spirit divine,
Tuned, open, accepting
The hand of my father.
Opportunities abound
To make a difference
To see, to appreciate, to compliment.
Wherever I am
I connect.
With a smile, a greeting,
The salutation:
"Make it a great day" and
The intent to do so myself.
My enthusiasm brings smiles,
Little moments of pleasure,
A more vivid, brighter day.

Acceptance

Upon the spiral of a life well lived
We meet the same lessons again and again.
In retreat we learn to let go of expectations
To receive what is given.
Take in the good and release what is left.
Memory does this naturally, with the passage of time.
Our memories tend to be happy remembrances
Of what was sacred, beautiful and connecting.
The lesson applies as well to loved ones.
Often disagreements arise
Out of desire to be heard, to be right.
If we can receive what is good
And witness the rest
Knowing our own worth
Loving and appreciating ourselves
Then it is easier to let it be
And appreciate the positive.
With loved ones
We would protect them from others
And protect others from their rough edges.
Doing so only adds fuel. Our part is to let go,
To honor the good, to allow loved ones
Their own path, without our corrections
Or explanations.

Dawn

What is the essence of this day?
The deep connection that will be made?
The sun loosens the skirts of night,
Pushes fingers of color across the sky.
Breathing deeply,
I open my eyes and my heart.
I listen to birds serenading the dawn.
Wrapped in tender feelings,
I begin to unfurl,
To kiss the joy as it flies,
Blissfully accepting this new day.

Possibility

I am unlimited potential. It is said, many reach less than 3% of their potential. I shall be a possibility thinker, wondering what might be possible, taking chances, reaching out, taking small steps, expanding the circle of my capabilities.

And beyond this, I shall be a "possibility base camp" for others, helping them see new possibilities, encouraging them to try it, to experiment, to see what happens.

Together, we will be more, do more, learn more. We will be aporia consultants to one another, sowing new ideas where there is doubt about how to begin. We will provide the support and encouragement that makes uncertainty no more than background noise.

In My Eyes

You can see who I am in my eyes,
In the way I smile,
In the things I say.

You can see who I am
When you listen to my poetry
When you are moved by my words

You can see who I am
When you invite me
To participate in what you love.

You can see who I am
By the way I seek opportunities
To make a difference.

You can see who I am
Only if you look,
Only if you care.

You can see who I am
In the same way that I see who you are,
By looking deep into your eyes.

By seeing the best within you
Knowing your possibilities, and
Letting you know that I know.

Showing The Way

When a man and a woman come together
Pledging their love, they become a partnership
Of possibility. Two unique expressions of love
Melding into one united front -
To serve, love and reach out to others.
Romance blesses the world.
Seeing the best in each other,
Supporting and encouraging each other
They see beauty, love, happiness and joy
Everywhere they look. And that expectation
Helps us all to walk with a lighter step,
To see the moment within the tensions
Of everyday life, to stop,
To breathe more deeply,
To see color more vibrantly.
When we return again to our own affairs,
Somehow a way through seems to appear,
The ability to take one more step
Into a brighter future.

A Brighter Vision

What is the highest possible vision
We, together, can hold of our relationship?
Each seeing ourselves in love,
Taking care of each other,
Amazed by this magnificent human being
Who has chosen to spend time with us.
We have taken on the task of
Enabling each to be all we can be,
Knowing that we will never walk alone,
For we have the greatest gift
In having found each other.

Cantadora

Stories are the links that draw us together,
That reveal our hearts, our commonalities,
Our need for love, understanding and connection.
The key I learned from my journaling
Lies in the pause.

As I listen, pause, wonder
Seek the essence, the nugget of value
I consider my own stories
Where the connections
To what I've learned lie.

My memories rise up
Stories that reveal the sacred me.
I share them and am pleased
To see recognition and appreciation
On the faces of new friends.

We grow to know each other
To find understanding,
To honor each others' strengths.
We develop new intimacy
The foundation for trust.

We hold our "trust" out carefully
A newborn fragility
And again we pause
Hoping to build tighter connections
To know love and loving.

Transformation

Taking interdependence to a new level
Namaste – seeing the divine in others
Together, united in belief, all things are possible.
Each committed to see the need where our passion
Leads us to serve, to be what we are prepared to be,
Taking one step at a time and knowing
That Spirit is at our back and
We cannot fail, if we follow
The path that has been prepared.
A light unto others, a sharing of delight, a presence.
A mastermind team of support and encouragement
For each others' passions.
We have come together,
Learned and grown.
We go forth fortified, encouraged, capable
Ready to make a difference
Each with our own unique gifts.

Making A Difference

Some folks say we get a better perspective on what we are about by considering what we would like others to say about us at our funeral. "Making a difference." Was #1 on my list.

Early on, I thought that making a difference had to be a huge endeavor, like solving world hunger. Then I learned that a service project is an opportunity to make a difference. I started collecting stories of people who are making this kind of a difference. One lady wrote a book and a blog about 10,000 service projects she took on in one year.

Then there was the book Random Acts of Kindness which reminds us to look for many little ways to make a difference every day. The movie "Pay It Forward" is one of my all time favorites. It espouses doing something for someone that they could not do themselves and asking them in turn to "pay it forward". Oprah took this on and gave a group of people each a sum of money to go out and find a way to "pay it forward". I would love to own a copy of that particular show.

A friend of mine was concerned that the girls in her daughter's school were not nice to each other, so she came up with her own "pay it forward" idea to make a difference. She tells groups of girls about her idea and gives them a small box with three hearts in it. As they find a way to "pay it forward" they give a heart with the deed and ask the recipient to "pay it forward" and pass the heart on. When all three hearts are given away they are invited to write a note about what happened and how they felt to my friend. She owns a store called "Precious Moments" and she hangs the stories on a tree limb in the store and sends the girl a heart necklace to keep.

So, it appears that "making a difference" is an ongoing journey, perhaps a spiritual path of listening and heeding, of becoming the hands of Spirit in serving one another.

Opportunities

What new possibilities will present themselves?
What needs can we meet
By reaching out, listening, participating, caring?
A smile, a thoughtful word,
A kind act
Can make all the difference,
Can turn the world around
For another and for us.
Suddenly we have lit up the morning,
Indeed, we have made it a great day
And this in only the first step.

Who Am I?

I am a child of God
Sent to hear his will
Following the pattern
Set by my elder brother.
Reading scriptures keeps me attuned, centered.
He wants me to be all that I can be
And to be that in service to others.
He wants me to see needs,
To recognize my own talents,
To put these together to solve problems.
Heavenly Father gave us families
To work together and learn together.
He put us in communities
To share and build understanding.
As communities touch,
We learn to hear each other,
To honor our commonalities,
To clarify the differences.
Yes, I am sent here to be all that I can be
To do those things he calls me to
And to practice making a difference
Until I am called back to his arms.

What I Know

I know I can make a difference.
I know that I am making choices
At every moment
And if each is an inch or two
Better, I will grow and learn and
Be more than I was.
This is called constant and
Never-ending improvement.
I know that I can be on the lookout
For random acts of kindness
That make others feel good.
I know that I can help
Wherever I see a need and
Ask others to "pay it forward".
I know that a smile
Can brighten a gloomy day,
A listening ear can lift a cloud and
Presence is the greatest gift of all
I know that love surrounds us and
We have only to open our eyes
In appreciation. Today,
I can make it a great day.

Second Naïveté

Abraham Maslow coined
The expression "second naïveté"
For those of us
Who choose to use
More of our potential,
To reach farther and higher,
To make a difference
For ourselves and others.
Long ago I was taught
That most people use
Less that 3% of their potential.
That day I set an intention
That my legacy
Would be that I always
Used more and more of my potential,
That I would explore, discover,
Expand, learn and grow.
Recently I read about
Being a "possibility base camp".
That has now become
A "barbarism" – a part
Of my very own "word hoard".
I not only seek more potential
For myself, but also to
Open the door to further possibilities
For others through my example,
My sharing and my connecting.

Trust

We live in a world of change, of ambiguity, of not knowing. I once had a very bright employee who had grown up in a rule bound black and white world and then gone into the Marine Corps where that kind of authoritarian rule structure was extolled. But our work was on the leading edge of an electronic technology where the closest you could get to his known experience was scientific hypothesis: where one dreamed up a plausible explanation and then rationally begin to test it. He did extremely well if he could be given the exact boundaries of a task and step-by-step directions.

These days we are learning more and more how to cope with "not knowing". I particularly like what I call the "MASH" analogy. As the team lived and worked in an atmosphere of near constant emergency, they were still able to play, to have fun, to indulge in humor and then when the next emergency came, change instantly to sharp team-aligned focus.

So I am learning to trust in the greater good, to seek the next step, to go into the silence and ask for direction.

Trust

Trust is a creative process
Trusting in the greater good.
The process unfolding.
I add faith and "practice."
I can, I must, I will
Make a difference.
"Make it a great day."
"I intend to."
Creation comes in
The actuation,
The choices we make,
The reaching out,
The discovery,
The love and energy we add.

Call And Response

Call

Heavenly Father
Out of my wildness
I cry unto thee.
Come close to me
Carry me across this place
With thee, I fear not.
Change me deeply
That I may be
The woman of your blueprint.
I lay this upon your altar
And walk away free.
Carry this burden.
Blow it away like chaff.
I would be more,
Closer to thee,
Trusting, whole, faithful
Seeing the footsteps
Where I am to follow.

Response

My precious child
Hold thyself
Wrapped in my love
And know your worth!
Stand tall and proud.
Give your gifts.
When you doubt
When you are uncertain
When you feel frustrated
Come unto me.
Rest in my arms
I will whisper love
Propose the next step.
We will do this together
Hand in hand.
You are deeply and
Completely acceptable

Courage

What is courage –
The art of standing tall
For your beliefs,
For what is important.
To stand by your heart.

Going deeper –
Courage takes hold
Of what is essential
And elusive
At the heart of an experience.

Then the task is
To follow the pulse
Of what matters
To be a guardian
Of what is not owned –

But must flow.
Letting relationships unfold.
Seeing how it all
Comes together,
As it is meant to be.

Following the questions
Into a deeper way of living.
Hearing the pulse of the sacred
Following the truth you hear, and
TRUSTING.

Just Because

May my quest for purpose be like a pebble
Dropped in the middle of this moment.
May silence be the foundation of essence
Releasing thoughts from the fist of my mind,
Carving space through the canyons of my bones.
As I move into the slow river of wonder
Skipping stones of good feeling across the water.
Let me rise from my solitude
To do something just because my heart sings "yes!"

Passion

Passion is what gets me out of bed in the morning. It is what drives me to be more, do more, reach for more. A good exercise might be to write a list: "I am passionate about…." My life goes more smoothly when I follow my passions, so it is interesting to consider how much time each of my passions gets over a week or a month. Then I can look at ways to allot more time to passions that are being short changed.

Often it is when a passion meets a need in another that the highest service can be offered. Stephen R. Covey calls this the "sweet spot" It is in a place like this, that we enter into flow, have a sense of timelessness.

Passion is the inhalation and produces exhalation that lifts a person and/or and event. And we all are blessed.

Passion

The central passion in my life
comes from my core, my essence.
I do not even know it
until I am quiet and
wait in attendance
to the silence.

The central passion in my life
Deals with building synergies
Helping others to see
their possibilities.
I want to be the base camp
for possibilities,
my own and those of others,
my friends, family and colleagues.

The central passion in my life
opens my heart to wider scenarios
shows me a higher perspective
a new way of seeing,
a new way of being.

The central passion in my life
Leads me to step out
To be all that I can be,
To recognize the woman I am becoming
And also to take the hand of those beside me
And show them what they can be,
What the possibilities are -
To encourage them in the choices they make.

Passionate

I feel passionate about

the natural beauty of each day,
my quiet hour of power each morning,
good books, inspiring thoughts
that expand my path, my clarity.

I feel passionate about

the woman I am becoming,
supporting those close to me,
being a base camp of possibilities,
making a difference.

I feel passionate about

learning and growth,
sharing and building synergies,
concepts that expand my horizons,
random acts of kindness.

I feel passionate about

opening my awareness,
noticing, paying attention,
seeking meaning, the essence,
accepting the jewels, releasing the rest.

Flow

Going With The Flow

Love is the key
The source of flow.
Think of a blessing
As an energy flow
From one to another.
Think of the flow
As a dance, a movement
Going on everywhere that we tap into.
Notice the synchronicities.
Feel the feelings
They engender.
As we move into flow
We build power
That explodes
Into synergies –
A greater good,
A greater possibility
Than before.

Wild Child

They say I should let my wild child out
I should try something new,
Like going to a Red Hat Convention,

Marching in a kazoo parade,
Writing new kinds of poetry.

The say today is the first day of the rest of my life,
Much awaits me
Like mountain retreats
Travel to Costa Rica
A service project in Appalachia.

They say that the best is yet to come
I should make a masterpiece of this day
By watching the sunrise
Walking in the sun,
Smiling at my neighbor

Becoming

Every day a new adventure,
An opportunity to be what I am,
To accept what is new,
To add a new layer, a new flavor
Through adventure, discovery,
Learning, listening, achieving.
To delight in whatever comes,
To go with the flow,
To indulge in life's treasures,
Smiling with delight,
Getting involved,
Becoming more,
Stretching and growing.
Wrapped in love.

Sacred Journey

Today is the first day
Of the rest of my life
I am consciously making choices
To enrich and deepen lives.
I am a catalyst, a celebrator.
I live a life rich with possibilities
Opportunities and options.
I am receiving the gifts others bring
Being touched by their lives.
My life is a dance of grace and gratitude.
Creativity opens me to the wonders
Of spontaneous change.
As intuitive insights pop up
I listen, take notice, learn and act.
Intuition is the juice for growing with the flow.

Meaning

As I have gotten older, meaning has become more important. Or has it? Even as a very young child I wanted to know why. I was full of questions. It is no wonder Mom wanted me to go play.

Being Pennsylvania Dutch, she would eventually say "Cat for to makes kitten's britches. Ever see them on puppy dogs?" That would stop me for a moment or two.

As I got older she would send me to an encyclopedia or even better (since it meant a bike ride) to the library. I loved the library. It was all rich woods with big, high windows and books everywhere.

With the internet and Wikipedia, we can find answers much more quickly.

But my search for meaning has advanced to more abstract areas. Now I turn more to reflection. I seek meaning from what happens. I seek the good parts, the joyful. I want to declare value in what is, to count my blessings, to continue to learn and grow.

Caught In The Quiet

The day is at its end
Intentions set
Seen through to completion
Tasks taken on,
Connections made,
Steps have moved us forward -
A good day
Errands run,
Good food shared,
Good words too.
Cleaning up,
Sitting quietly
With our tea.
Listening to chimes
And a fountain.
Caught in the quiet.
End of another lovely day,
Laying our heads down
To a peaceful sleep.

A Peony

What flower is like an onion
With layers upon layers?
Perhaps a peony.

We are all flowers
Opening up a layer at a time
Learning new lessons
Considering possibilities
Soaking up meaning
Like summer sunshine.
We let old petals
Like old ways of being
Drift into forgetfulness.

What bits of wisdom
Shall I extract from this day
To put upon the altar
Of my life as symbols
Of new possibility?

So Much Happiness

It is difficult to know what to do
With so much happiness.
Delight arises from the moment,
Skims across the lake.
You want to dance,
To sing and shout "Yes",
Lay on the grass,
Watch the clouds dance,
Listen to the breeze sing
Through the trees,
Smile deep inside
Satisfied with what is.
Let your happiness caress you.
Float beyond and infect all those you touch.

Definitions

Meaning is a shady edifice
Influenced by the lost past.
We are capable of only fractured perceptions
Built from hatreds, injuries, scraps,
Uplifted by small victories and bits of conversation
Which amalgamate into symbols to live by.
Here we take our stand.
Finding common ground
In the expanded expression
Of our definitions,
We re-describe the world
A first step in changing it,
Increasing the sum of what is possible.

Yes I Can

I am a cock-eyed optimist
I build base-camps for possibilities.
I expect miracles.
I sing and dance through my worries.

I draw faces on the pain.
I know the roller coaster of life
Will soon be racing for another high
And I will scream for the sheer joy of it all.

I laugh at the clouds,
Kick the snow into puffs
Warm my hands by the fire's glow
and with a hot cup of cocoa.

I smile at my mistakes,
Learn the lessons,
Look for deeper meanings,
Let it all go.

Connecting

It appears to me that connecting is what life is all about, getting to know each other, telling our stories. But, even more, laughing and playing together.

My brother and I would climb on our parents' bed on Sunday mornings and they would tickle us. I loved tickling and wrestling and climbing over each other.

Later we played "pretend" games with other children. And by our teen years we were into talk, discussing it all with each other, learning from each other. There was so much to learn and so little time.

Then there were high school clubs centered around sports, drama, music and even language clubs. We centered our friendships, our connections around topics.

Now I value those who are not like me, those who have different perspectives and can widen my lens. I want to know more and do more.

I have been taught that more ideas give us better options so we can make better choices.

I love teaming, deep conversations, collaborations, building synergies, supporting and encouraging one another, and helping each other make a difference.

I like new, larger possibilities. I want to be open to more possibilities and to be a "base camp" of possibilities for others.

Kindness

I do not have to lose things to know what kindness is.
I have felt the future dissolve
In a moment…. Disasters do this.
So do people. The heart of what
I am is connection.
Connections can bring hurt.
But they also bring the deepest of joys.
Often one following the other.
In losing, we learn to listen, to come together,
To bind each others' wounds,
To release self-pity with the filling of needs,
To stand at attention before
The "tao" of existence,
Open to God's wonderful surprises.

Beyond Our Human-Ness

When will we learn
to take the world as it is given,
to step beyond rooms of selfhood,
watch the new day unfold?

Always time goes rushing
beyond the moment.
We miss the great and sunny squares,
the fountains teased by light.

Our friends are not perfect
speaking with tongues of gold.
They hide when heavens thunder,
flawed, human, asking for more.

Yet, it is in touch,
moments of connection,
that we learn to accept
to more fully appreciate.

To accept our human –ness
And love even more
Because beyond who we seem,
We are love and laughter and light.

We are learning how to see more
How to do more
How to reach
For all that we can be.

One More Step

I am the synergist, the gateway to possibility.
Together we look beyond the day.
We connect and leverage
Looking at other perspectives,
Designing, planning, developing.
Taking quantum leaps into the future.
We thrive on dreams and laughter and possibilities
And end the day having put another footstep
Into the path others will follow.

When Spirits Dance

I am a bright little spirit
Wandering wooded trails
Stopping to admire a wild violet.
Warmed by slanting rays of sunlight,
Other spirits wander here
When we meet we dance and laugh
With eyes shining
We pass around the neat little packages
Of our accomplishments and share our successes.
We are refreshed, knowing
We can, we will.
Skipping off to new adventures.

Appreciation

Appreciation is the icing on the cake. It adds sweetness to the event. Recently I read about a new way to do a Gratitude Journal. It is called "100 Gratitudes". The author asks us to add another step. Write a gratitude. Then give a reason why you are grateful for this. For example I am grateful for my "pied-a-terre" in West Virginia. It is a place to slow down, to relax, to let go, to read and ponder and enjoy nature.

My motto for this year is "Accept, Appreciate, Celebrate". To take what is, find ways to appreciate and then celebrate what I have found. Isn't that a great formula?

Wayne Dyer teaches us to separate facts from projections, seek the bigger picture, appreciate, then share our joy with others with positive acts on their behalf. He was able to do this even when in the hospital recovering from a heart attack.

Wonder

How do I measure the beauty of this day?
The sun climbs smiling above the horizon.
The birds begin their morning rituals.
Heavenly Father has given us another beautiful day.
Early morning hours to think and pray and choose
Tasks to perform, people to help
Strategies to plan.
My son has lifted my heart with an invitation.
He wants my husband and I
To join his family for a weekend on the beach.
First there is the drive on a clear day,
Time for discussions and sharing
Time for good books and good music
Time to release day-to-day worries,
Chores, problems, tasks.
We are out, being reminded
Of this amazing earth, of trees and flowers,
Breezes and waves,
Opportunities to share, to laugh,
To enjoy each other,
Of the delight of childhood,
Knowing what you want,
Going for it, enjoying the process.

What Have I Given

I am given everything:
Air to breathe, feet to walk
Eyes to see, arms to feel.
I am asked only to appreciate,
To receive, to savor, to share.
To give laughter and smiles,
Moments of connection and appreciation.
I am asked to remember
That in my words, smiles, laughter
I am giving.
I am expected to delight
In the patience of the blue heron
In the mirror like surface
Of tannin stained swamp waters,
To mirror the wolf's delight
At feeding time, his joy
In the presence of his caretaker,
To take and consider
The lessons of nature,
To learn from all creatures.

Words Of Wisdom

How shall I inhale this whole day?
With my eyes, with my breath,
With my attention, my love, my reaching out.
I inhale this day with my first breaths
With my smiles, with my prayers
With my listening, with my heart.
I inhale this day with my first steps,
Opening the door, seeing the sidewalk,
The grass, the flowers, the trees,
When I raise my eyes to sunrise colors
And feel the breezes
Of another beautiful day.
I inhale this day with every greeting,
Every smile, every thoughtful act,
Every appreciative word, every dream.
I inhale this day with every challenge,
Every opportunity to excel.
And I inhale this day yet again
When I think back and look deep
At meanings, discoveries, learnings
And say "Thank-you."

Endpiece

The Woman I Am Becoming

Now I am becoming all
I am meant to be.
Its taken time, many years,
Many places. Now to stand still,
To revel in the silence.
My poems, my words
Shape the shaper.
All fuses, falls into place
From thought to desire to action.
I watch, reflect, enjoy, savor
My work, my loves, my time, my place
Gathered into one intense me,
Made so and rooted so by love.

Based on a May Sarton poem